YOUR FAVORITE STARS

FEATURING

SHAWN MENDES

FACTS, QUIZZES, ACTIVITIES, AND MORE!

by Erin Falligant

T0413382

CAPSTONE PRESS
a capstone imprint

This is an unauthorized biography.

Published by Capstone Press, an imprint of Capstone
1710 Roe Crest Drive, North Mankato, Minnesota 56003
capstonepub.com

Library of Congress Cataloging-in-Publication Data
Names: Falligant, Erin, author.
Title: Featuring Shawn Mendes : facts, quizzes, activities, and more / by Erin Falligant.
Description: North Mankato, Minnesota : Brain Candy Books, an imprint of Capstone Press, 2025. | Series: Your favorite stars | Audience: Ages 8-11 | Audience: Grades 4-6 | Summary: "How long did it take for Shawn Mendes's first EP to reach number one on iTunes? How many shows did he perform for his 2019 worldwide tour? Which of Shawn's tattoos was inspired by fan suggestions, celebrating his album *Illuminate*? Fans can read about all this and more in this collection of fun facts, photos, and more, featuring the hit singer-songwriter!"— Provided by publisher.
Identifiers: LCCN 2024057245 (print) | LCCN 2024057246 (ebook) | ISBN 9798875233098 (hardcover) | ISBN 9798875233043 (paperback) | ISBN 9798875233050 (pdf) | ISBN 9798875233067 (epub) | ISBN 9798875233074 (kindle edition)
Subjects: LCSH: Mendes, Shawn, 1998-—Miscellanea—Juvenile literature. | Mendes, Shawn, 1998-—Juvenile literature.
Classification: LCC ML3930.M444 F35 2025 (print) | LCC ML3930.M444 (ebook) | DDC 782.42164092—dc23/eng/20241209
LC record available at https://lccn.loc.gov/2024057245
LC ebook record available at https://lccn.loc.gov/2024057246

Editorial Credits
Editor: Julie Gassman; Designer: Elyse White; Media Researcher: Rebekah Hubstenberger; Production Specialist: Tori Abraham

TABLE OF
CONTENTS

CHAPTER 1

GET TO KNOW SHAWN

quiz! TRUE OR FALSE

Test your Shawn Mendes IQ!
Is each statement true or false?

1. Shawn was born in Portugal.

2. He has two middle names: "Peter" and "Raul."

3. Shawn has two younger sisters.

4. He played Prince Charming in a high school play.

5. Shawn didn't finish high school because he started touring.

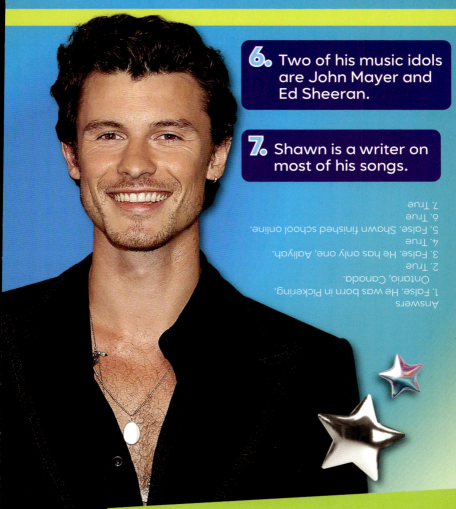

6. Two of his music idols are John Mayer and Ed Sheeran.

7. Shawn is a writer on most of his songs.

Answers
1. False. He was born in Pickering, Ontario, Canada.
2. True
3. False. He has only one, Aaliyah.
4. True
5. False. Shawn finished school online.
6. True
7. True

HOW'D YOU DO?

6-7 correct: **TOP FAN**
4-5 correct: **TUNED IN**
1-3 correct: **MORE TO LEARN (READ ON!)**

A BOY AND HIS GUITAR

Shawn grew up in **Pickering**, a town near Toronto, Canada. At 13, he taught himself how to play guitar by watching YouTube tutorials. He also watched videos of people covering songs, or performing songs by other musicians. Shawn posted videos of himself covering songs by Adele, Hunter Hayes, and Rihanna—and fans tuned in. His cover of Justin Bieber's "**As Long as You Love Me**" went viral overnight!

STAR SCOOP!

Shawn is a Potterhead. As a kid, he made his own wands out of sticks. He says he would have been sorted into Gryffindor at Hogwarts, just like Harry.

A young Shawn performs at a concert back in 2014.

SHAWN'S FAVORITE THINGS

THE NUMBER 8

A STUFFED LION NAMED LEO

GUITARS—HE HAS MORE THAN 40!

MEANINGFUL TATTOOS

THE COLOR BLUE

ELEPHANTS

HANGING OUT WITH FRIENDS AND FAMILY IN CANADA

GAME OF THRONES

STAR SCOOP!

Shawn and Justin Bieber have a lot in common. They both rose to fame in their early teens, and they're both Canadian! While Shawn grew up in Pickering, Justin grew up two hours away in Stratford, Ontario.

SUPER SIBS

Shawn's little sister, **Aaliyah**, is five years younger, but they've always been close. In fact, he owes some of his success to his little sis. Aaliyah recorded most of the early videos that Shawn posted online! Shawn carves out time to spend with his sister, whom he now considers a close friend. He even has her name, "**AALIYAH MARIA**," tattooed under his collarbone.

STAR SCOOP!

Aaliyah is a bit of a celebrity too. She has more than 750,000 followers on Instagram!

CHAPTER 2

FINDING THE WORDS

Shawn called his first album *Handwritten* because he wrote or cowrote every song, many of them by hand on notepads. He writes songs about his life, like his rise to fame and his relationship with onetime girlfriend Camila Cabello. For his 2024 album, *Shawn*, he wrote about the anxiety he has dealt with over the last few years. Shawn isn't afraid to open up and be honest with his fans through his music.

Camila Cabello

quiz!

FIND THE RIGHT WORDS

Can you complete the lyrics to some of Shawn's well-known songs?

1. "My _____ still shaking
My mind's still racing
My heart's still breaking in two"

A. body's
B. skeleton's
C. hand's

2. "I know I can treat you better than he can
And any girl like you deserves _____"

A. a gentleman
B. a decent man
C. an adoring fan

3. "But what if I, what if I trip?
What if I, what if I fall?
Then am I _____ ?"

    A. the loser
    B. the monster
    C. the klutz

4. "Help me, it's like the walls are caving in
Sometimes I feel like giving up
No _____ is strong enough"

    A. superhero
    B. medicine
    C. titanium

STAR SCOOP!

Shawn's father encouraged him to write songs. When Shawn said he wanted to be a writer but didn't know if he could do it, his father said, "Go write a song." So he did!

1. C (from "Isn't That Enough," 2024), 2. A (from "Treat You Better," 2016), 3. B (from "Monster" with Justin Bieber, 2020), 4. B (from "In My Blood," 2018)

WHAT INSPIRES SHAWN'S SONGS?

"**Three Empty Words**" may have been inspired by a relationship ending. "**Mercy**" is thought to be about the music industry that Shawn wished would give him time to breathe. "**In My Blood**" was about overcoming anxiety. After losing a childhood friend, Shawn wrote "**Heart of Gold**" to work through his sadness. Whatever the inspiration, Shawn always writes straight from the heart.

STAR SCOOP!

Shawn canceled most of his tour, *Wonder: The World Tour*, in 2022. He took two years off to take care of his mental health. He next returned to the stage on August 8, 2024—his 26th birthday!

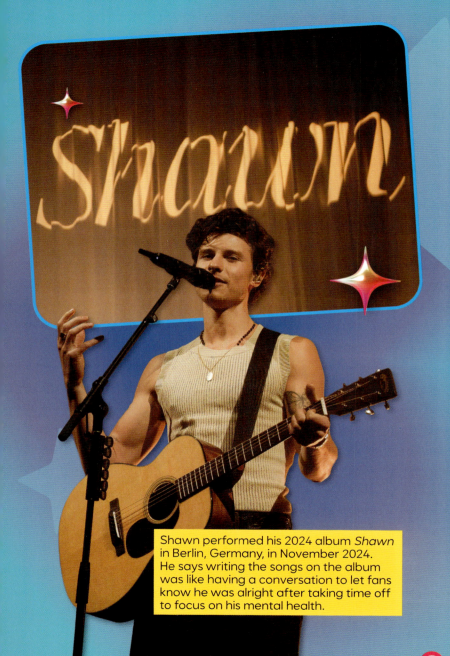

Shawn performed his 2024 album *Shawn* in Berlin, Germany, in November 2024. He says writing the songs on the album was like having a conversation to let fans know he was alright after taking time off to focus on his mental health.

BE THE SONGWRITER!

Want to write your own lyrics to one of Shawn's melodies? Print out his lyrics, and follow these steps to write your own:

1. Pick a topic that fits the mood of the tune. If it's a love song, write about a person or pet you love. Is the song sad? Silly? Pick a topic that matches that mood.

2. Write down rhyming words that have to do with your topic. If your topic is "my cat," rhyming words might be *fur* and *purr*, or *paws* and *claws*.

3. Come up with a chorus, or the part of your song that will repeat. Use rhyming words to write lines that are about the same length as the lyrics in Shawn's chorus, such as:

I love your whiskers and your soft fur.
I love to cuddle and hear you purr.

4. Come up with a few verses, or the parts of the song that tell a story about your topic. For a song about cats, you might write about meeting a kitty at a shelter or about how your cat got its name.

5. Start with verse 1, then sing the chorus. Write verse 2, and repeat your chorus. Can you think of a third verse? If not, repeat your chorus again to finish the song.

6. Look up an instrumental version of the song online, and use *your* lyrics to sing along!

CHAPTER 3

FROM STUDIO TO STAGE

STAR SCOOP!

When Shawn released *The Shawn Mendes EP*, a collection of his first four songs, it took only 37 minutes for it to reach number one on iTunes! Since then, he has recorded five full albums.

SHAWN'S ALBUMS

HANDWRITTEN (2015)—HIT NUMBER ONE ON THE *BILLBOARD* 200 CHART AFTER ONLY ONE WEEK

ILLUMINATE (2016)—NAMED FOR THE WAY MUSIC CAN BE A LIGHT DURING DARK TIMES

SHAWN MENDES (2018)—INSPIRED BY ED SHEERAN, JUSTIN TIMBERLAKE, ONEREPUBLIC, AND JOHN MAYER

WONDER (2020)—INCLUDES A SONG RECORDED WITH JUSTIN BIEBER

SHAWN (2024)—WRITTEN AND RECORDED ALL ACROSS THE U.S. AND COSTA RICA

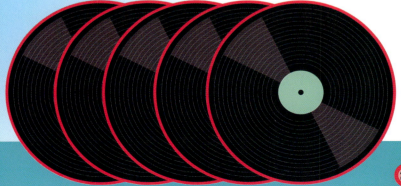

TAKING IT ON THE ROAD

Shawn enjoys promoting his albums and connecting with fans on the road. He has done four world tours and taken to the stage with many fellow musicians, including Taylor Swift, Ed Sheeran, and Justin Bieber. Shawn says that performing in front of crowds feels **"like your feet are floating off the ground. It's kind of pure magic from start to finish."**

STAR SCOOP!

Taylor Swift and 60,000 fans sang "Happy Birthday" to Shawn on his seventeenth birthday! Taylor invited him onstage while they were performing in Seattle, Washington.

SHAWN AROUND THE WORLD!

Shawn's biggest tour to date was his Shawn Mendes: The Tour 2019 world tour. He performed 105 shows in only nine months. Check out his route!

NORTH AMERICA
53 SHOWS

TOUR ENDED IN NORTH AMERICA ON DECEMBER 21, 2019

SOUTH AMERICA
7 SHOWS

TOUR STARTED IN EUROPE ON MARCH 7, 2019

EUROPE
27 SHOWS

ASIA
9 SHOWS

AUSTRALIA AND NEW ZEALAND
9 SHOWS

FOR FRIENDS AND FAMILY ONLY

To promote *Shawn*, his fifth album, Shawn performed a "**For Friends and Family Only**" tour that featured performances in small theaters in just nine cities. Shawn says he "wanted the first shows back to be special" and to play the album live in some of the places he recorded it. It was the only time Shawn has performed an entire album live from top to bottom!

STOPS ON THE TOUR:

WOODSTOCK   BROOKLYN   MORRISON, CO

LONDON   LOS ANGELES   BERLIN

NASHVILLE   SEATTLE   TORONTO

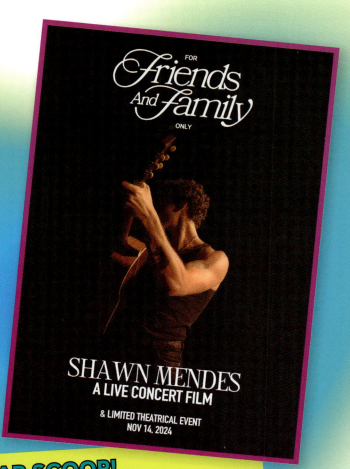

FOR
Friends
And *Family*
ONLY

SHAWN MENDES
A LIVE CONCERT FILM

& LIMITED THEATRICAL EVENT
NOV 14, 2024

STAR SCOOP!

To make sure that all of Shawn's fans could enjoy the performance, the *For Friends and Family Only (A Live Concert Film)* movie was shown in theaters on November 14, 2024.

CHAPTER 4

FEELING THE LOVE

Shawn has always relied on his fans, called the "**Mendes Army**," to spread the word about his music. When Shawn released his first single, "*Life of the Party*," on iTunes, it jumped to number one in minutes—without ever being played on the radio. It was advertised only on social media! And he never forgets the followers who made him famous. He makes time to take photos and hold meet and greets with fans after concerts.

STAR SCOOP!

Shawn got his start on YouTube and Vine, but as of 2024, Shawn had nearly 72 million followers on Instagram!

FORGIVING FANS

During his 2019 world tour, Shawn had to cancel a show in Rio de Janeiro, Brazil. His vocal cords were swollen from a sinus infection and months of performing, and doctors warned him against singing—or even talking. Shawn apologized to fans online. He hated to let them down!

Then he heard chanting from outside his hotel window and saw about 2,000 fans gathered in the street below. Instead of being angry, they had turned out to support him! Shawn said:

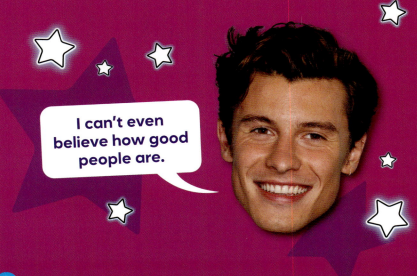

I can't even believe how good people are.

STAR SCOOP!

Shawn asked fans to help him design a tattoo to celebrate his *Illuminate* album. Many fans suggested a lightbulb image and the color blue. Three weeks later, Shawn revealed his new tattoo: a lightbulb full of blue orchids.

WHAT SHAWN LEARNED FROM...

JOHN MAYER:

"The most incredible thing I've learned from him is that you are never a master of something. John Mayer is literally the best guitarist in the world . . . and he would text me asking what I think about a song."

TAYLOR SWIFT:

"I learned [from Taylor] what it meant to be a performer, and it wasn't about being perfect. It was about enjoying it. Because you watch someone on stage, whatever they're doing, and if they are truly enjoying themselves, so are you."

ED SHEERAN:

"Ed Sheeran gave me some really awesome advice and showed me how real everything is gonna be. . . . He helped me to keep my calm. He knew how crazy it would be before I even knew."

STAR SCOOP!

Shawn was once a fanboy too. He looked up to John Mayer, Ed Sheeran, and Bruno Mars. When Shawn won the 2017 American Music Award for Favorite Male Adult Contemporary Artist, he actually beat out Ed Sheeran and Bruno Mars!

CHAPTER 5

MORE THAN A MUSICIAN

Shawn has lots to keep him busy beyond his music. One area of interest is acting. Before he ever even started singing, he wanted to be an actor. And he became one! He voiced characters in two children's movies and earned a spot on one of his favorite television shows, *The 100*.

STAR SCOOP!

Shawn was a big fan of the television shows *Lost* and *Grey's Anatomy*.

SHAWN MENDES STARRED AS...

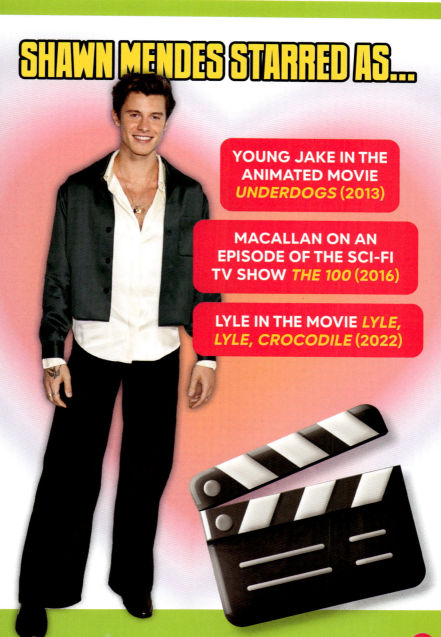

YOUNG JAKE IN THE ANIMATED MOVIE *UNDERDOGS* (2013)

MACALLAN ON AN EPISODE OF THE SCI-FI TV SHOW *THE 100* (2016)

LYLE IN THE MOVIE *LYLE, LYLE, CROCODILE* (2022)

GOOD SCENTS

One of Shawn's first business ventures outside of music was to create his own cologne in 2017. **SHAWN MENDES SIGNATURE** cologne smells like fruits, flowers, musk, and maple syrup—something Canada, Shawn's home country, is known for.

Shawn loved cologne even as a kid. "When I was seven or eight, my dad would spray cologne and I would run through it," he says. Where did he advertise his cologne? On Instagram, of course!

STAR SCOOP!

The box for Shawn's cologne features a guitar that was inspired by Shawn's first tattoo. The guitar is made up of trees reflecting on water, the skyline of Toronto, and a soundwave of his family saying "I love you."

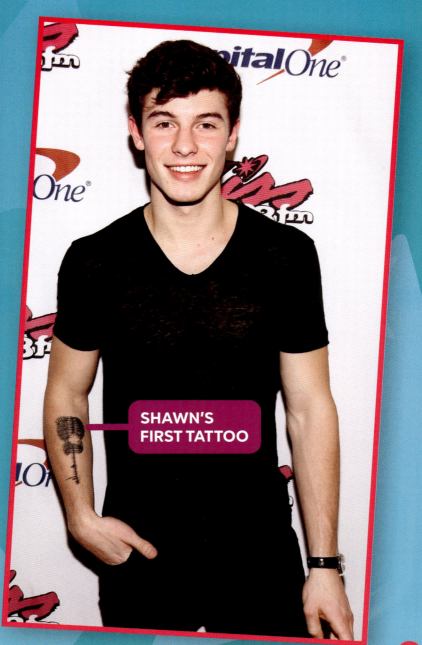

SHAWN'S FIRST TATTOO

THE FACE OF FASHION

Shawn's good looks caught the eye of a modeling agency named **WILHELMINA**. He signed on with the agency in 2016 and walked the runway at Men's Fashion Week in Milan, Italy, in 2017.

Shawn soon became the face of some big brands. **ARMANI** chose Shawn to help boost sales of their "Connected" smartwatch collection, and **CALVIN KLEIN** chose him to represent their brand in 2019. Shawn's Instagram post of him wearing Calvin Kleins was one of his most popular. Within two days, the post had 8 million likes!

♥ **8 MILLION**

Shawn teamed up with Tommy Hilfiger for a collection of sustainable fashion called Tommy X Shawn Classics Reborn.

STAR SCOOP!

Shawn isn't the only model in the family. When he had a photo shoot for Tommy Hilfiger clothing in 2023, his little sister, Aaliyah, came too!

CHAPTER 6

GIVING BACK

Whether Shawn is making music or modeling, he tries to give back to fans and be a role model. In 2014, he started the "**#NOTESFROMSHAWN**" campaign with DoSomething.org. He wanted to help people dealing with sadness and low self-esteem by inviting fans and followers to write positive notes. The messages, written on sticky tags, were posted in random public places to spread kindness. In the first year, more than 53,000 people took part and wrote nearly 260,000 notes!

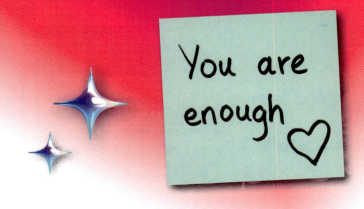

STAR SCOOP!

Shawn spreads hope and raises funds through fashion. As ambassador for David Yurman jewelry in 2023, he helped design a woven hemp bracelet to raise money for charity.

INSPIRING OTHERS

Shawn created the Shawn Mendes Foundation to inspire youth to speak up for issues they care about. The foundation awards **"WONDER GRANTS"** to young people with big ideas for how to help others, improve education, or protect the environment. Since the first Wonder Grant was given in 2020, more than 30 grants have been awarded! Some have been given to support children's mental health, a cause that Shawn himself is passionate about.

STAR SCOOP!

Shawn says music is like therapy for him, and he hopes it will also help others. His foundation donated a million dollars to fund music therapy for kids at Toronto's Hospital for Sick Children!

Author and motivational speaker Fanta Ballo was awarded the first Wonder Grant. The grant helped Ballo finish her book of poetry.

WONDER GRANTS CATEGORIES:

- ANTI-BULLYING
- MUSIC TECH ACCESS
- ECOSYSTEMS
- POETRY
- EDUCATION
- RACIAL JUSTICE
- HUMAN RIGHTS
- SUSTAINABILITY
- MENTAL HEALTH
- SUSTAINABILITY—WATER
- YOUTH EMPOWERMENT

FIVE MORE WAYS SHAWN HAS GIVEN BACK

RAISED MONEY TO BUILD A **SCHOOL IN GHANA** (2015)

STARTED A **FUNDRAISER FOR VICTIMS** OF AN EARTHQUAKE IN MEXICO (2017)

WROTE A SONG AND DONATED PROCEEDS TO **HELP FIGHT GUN VIOLENCE** (2018)

PERFORMED AT A BENEFIT TO **FIGHT POVERTY IN NEW YORK** (2019)

DONATED MONEY TO **FIGHT THE SPREAD OF COVID-19** (2020)

Shawn helped spread the word about a Global Climate Strike march, calling for action to protect the environment. Fans responded by marching with Shawn Mendes-themed signs.

STAR SCOOP!

Shawn cares about the climate. He partnered with Reverb.org to make his 2022 Wonder tour more eco-friendly, including eating local food, cleaning buses with green products, and encouraging fans to bring their own water bottles to shows!

BE LIKE SHAWN. SPREAD POSITIVITY!

You don't have to be a famous musician to make the world a better place. Take a page from Shawn and spread kindness in your own community. Here's how:

- Find a pad of colorful sticky notes.

- Brainstorm kind messages to write on the notes, such as "You're amazing," "Somebody loves you," and "You can change the world with your smile."

- Post the notes in random places, such as on mirrors in public restrooms, on magazines in checkout lanes, or on lockers at school.

- Encourage your friends to do the same!

YOU can change the world, one sticky note at a time.

ABOUT THE AUTHOR

Erin Falligant has written more than 50 books for children. Her Joss series for American Girl, written about a young surfer with hearing loss, earned a 2020 Moonbeam Gold Medal Award. Erin draws from her master's degree in child clinical psychology to write advice books on changing bodies, standing up to bullies, making friends, and mastering mindfulness. To learn more about Erin and her books, visit www.erinfalligant.com

READ MORE ABOUT YOUR FAVORITE STARS

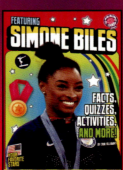

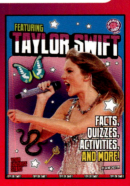